B

Classical *for* Guitar

Table of Contents

Copyright © MCMXCVI by Alfred Publishing Co., Inc.
All rights reserved.   Printed in USA.

ISBN 0-88284-965-4

Music engraving: Nancy Butler
Production editor: L. C. Harnsberger

in **TAB**

How to Use This Book

Classical for Guitar in TAB contains ten selections from the standard guitar repertoire by Carcassi, Carulli, Giuliani, Sor and Tárrega and seven transcriptions of Bach, Paganini, Pachelbel and Beethoven. The music spans 250 years. The solos were selected for their proven appeal to students as well as their value for technical development. They represent a variety of grades or difficulties.

About the Grading: The grading is based on the system set forth by the ASTA (American String Teachers Association) Guitar Division. The grading is as follows:

grade 1 Short selections; two-part texture or basic arpeggio patterns; a minimum of simple slurs; no barres; first position only.

grade 2 Mainly two-part texture or arpeggio patterns with greater thumb movement than in grade one; simple shifts between first and second position; slurs; no full barres.

grade 3 Chordal textures in common keys; some upper positions in conjunction with open-string basses only; half-barres for short periods; simple shifts with guide fingers only.

grade 4 More extended pieces; more difficult position shifts; full barre for short periods in simple fingerings.

Each piece is arranged in three ways: 1) standard classical guitar notation with right-hand techniques (*p = thumb, i = index, m = middle finger, a = ring finger*); 2) chord frames above the music indicating the left-hand position and fingerings; 3) tablature below the standard music notation indicating exactly where on the fingerboard the notes are to be played.

Tablature Explanation

Tablature is a system of notation that graphically represents the strings and frets of the guitar fingerboard. Each note is indicated by placing a number, which indicates the fret or finger position to be picked, on the appropriate string. For example:

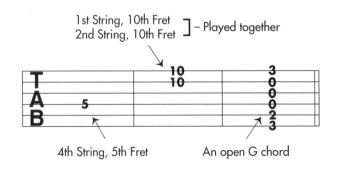

1st String, 10th Fret
2nd String, 10th Fret] – Played together

4th String, 5th Fret   An open G chord

Andantino

Mateo Carcassi (1792–1853)

Waltz

Ferdinando Carulli (1770–1841)

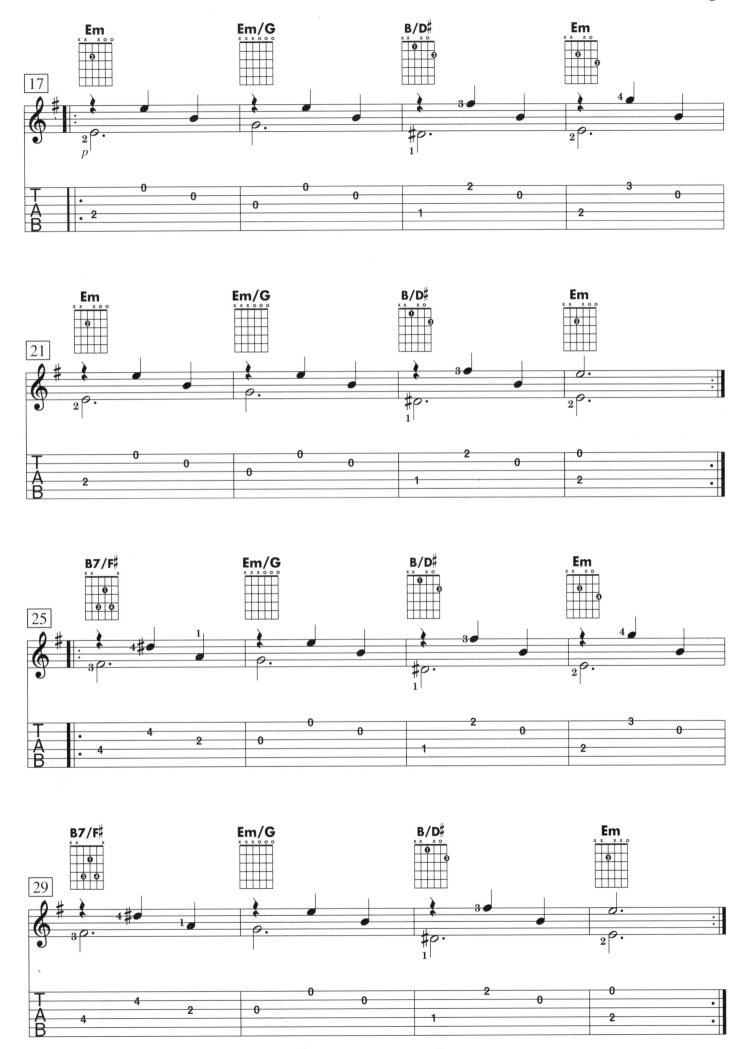

Andante

Fernando Sor (1778–1839)

Andante

Ferndando Carulli (1770–1841)

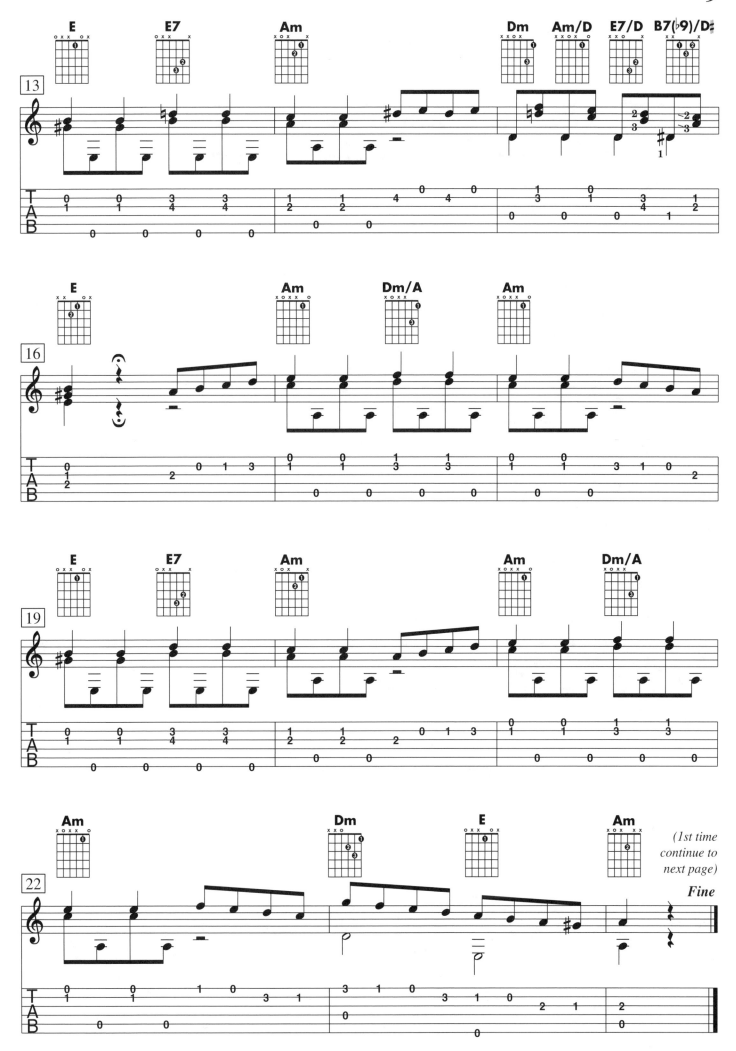

(1st time
continue to
next page)

Fine

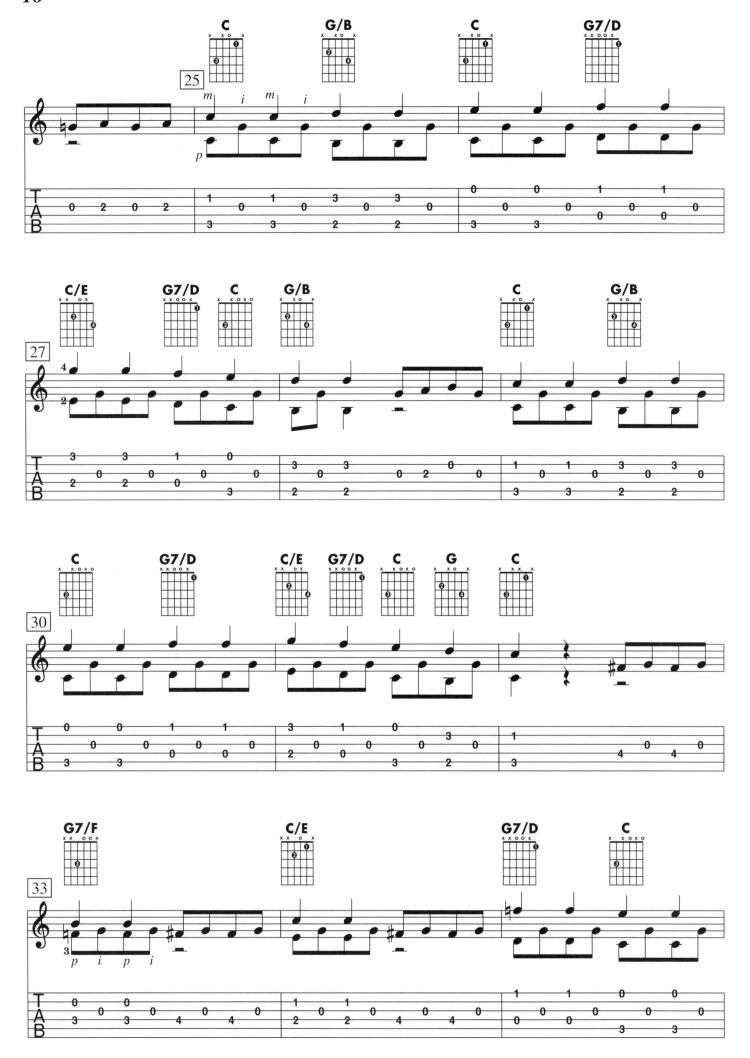

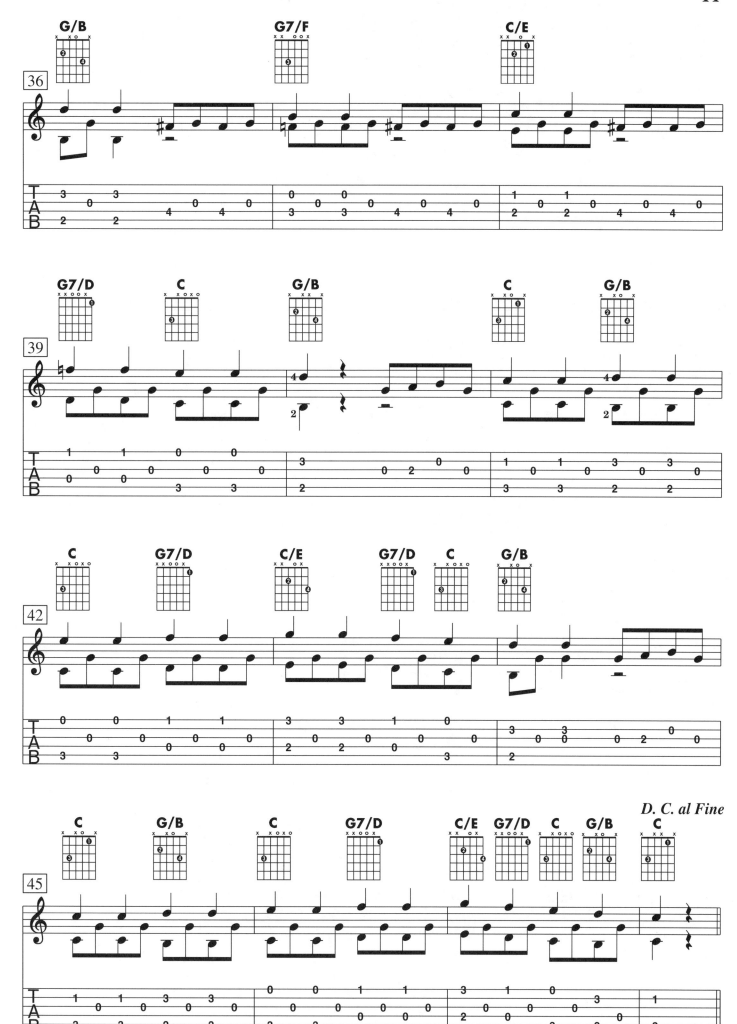

D. C. al Fine

Study

Ferdinando Carulli (1770–1841)

Allegro

Mauro Giuliani (1781–1829)

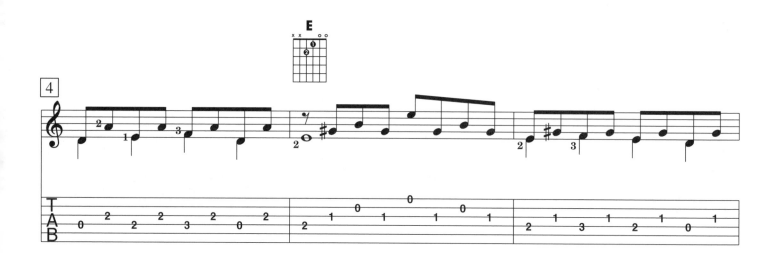

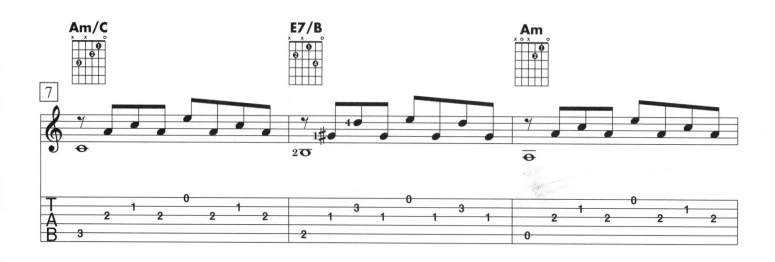

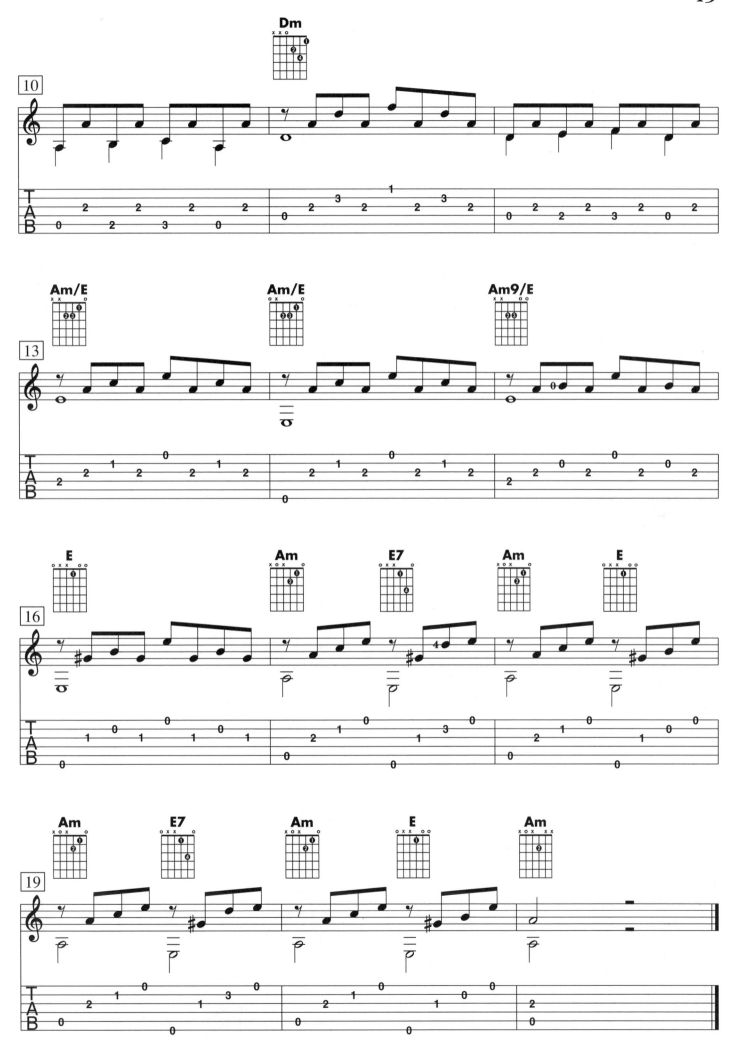

Für Elise

Ludwig van Beethoven (1770–1827)

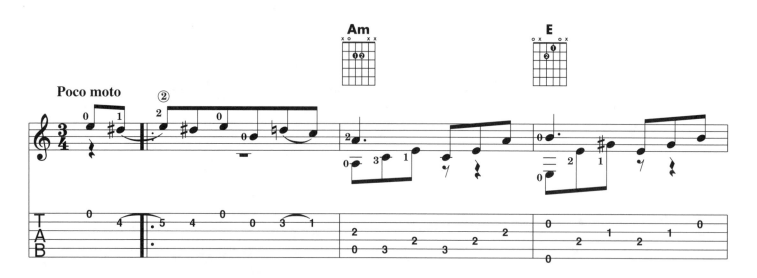

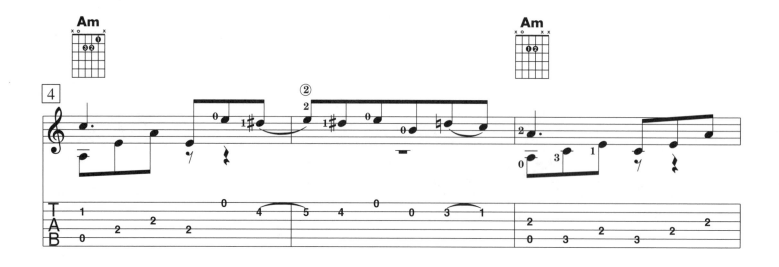

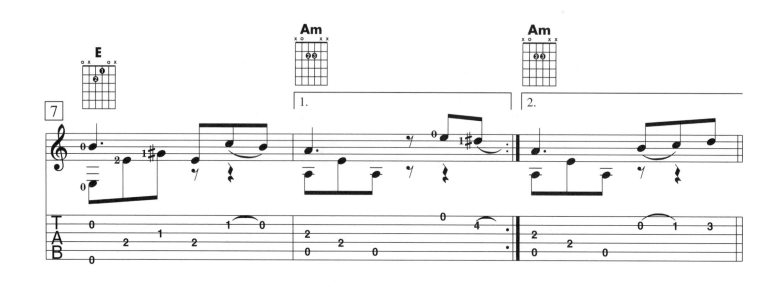

Study in E Minor

Francisco Tárrega (1852–1909)

Prelude

Johann Sebastian Bach (1685–1750)
from Cello Suite No. 1

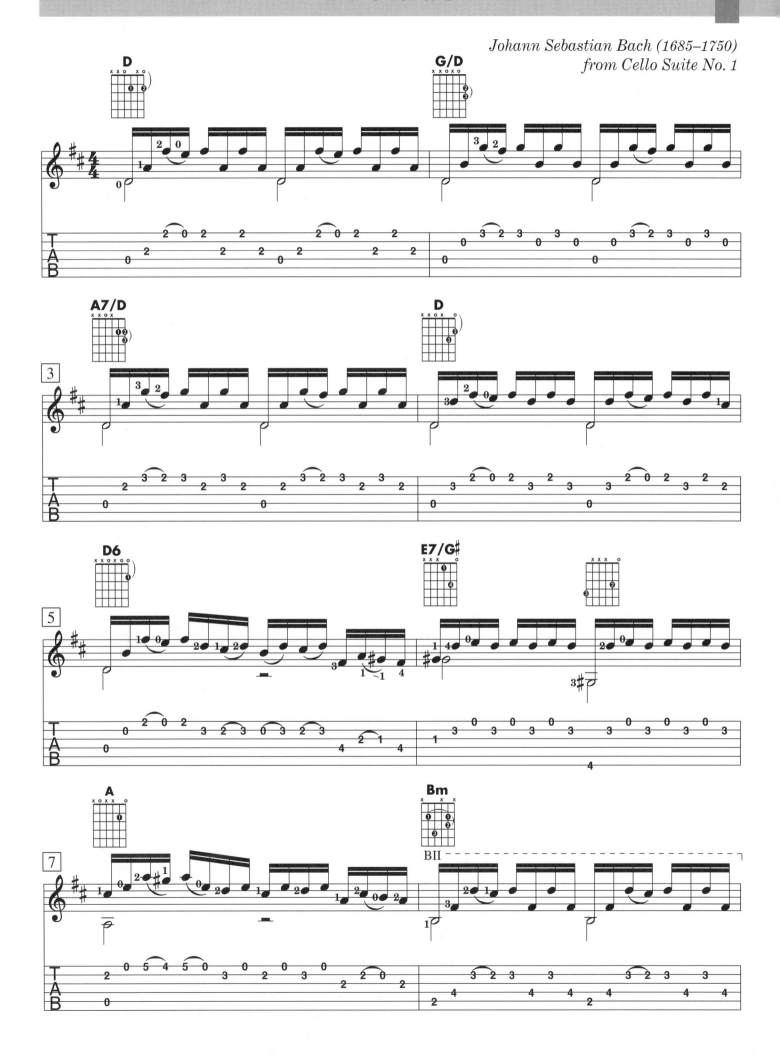

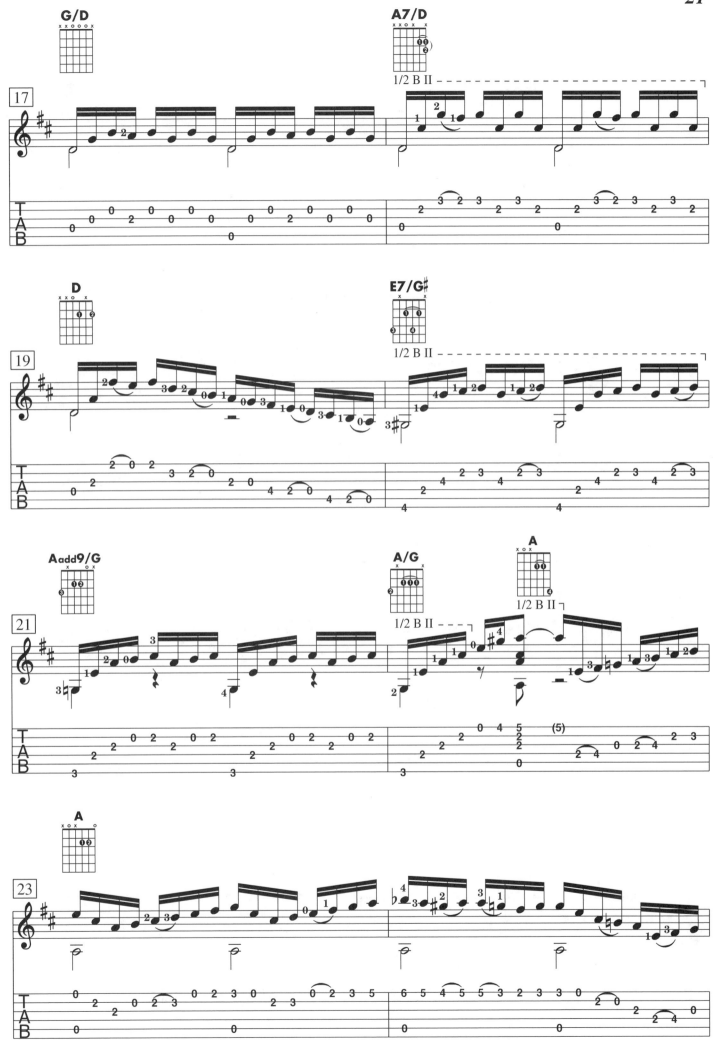

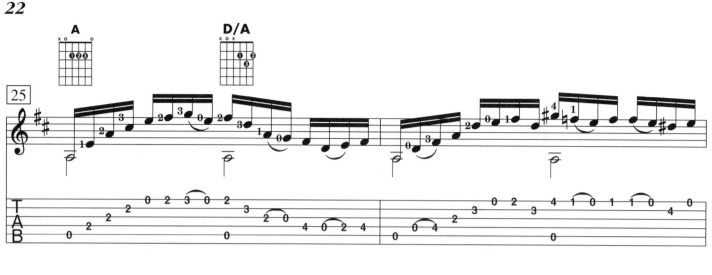

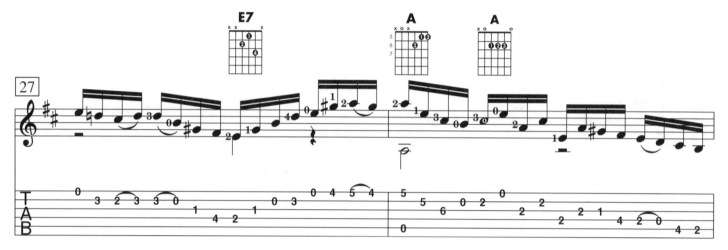

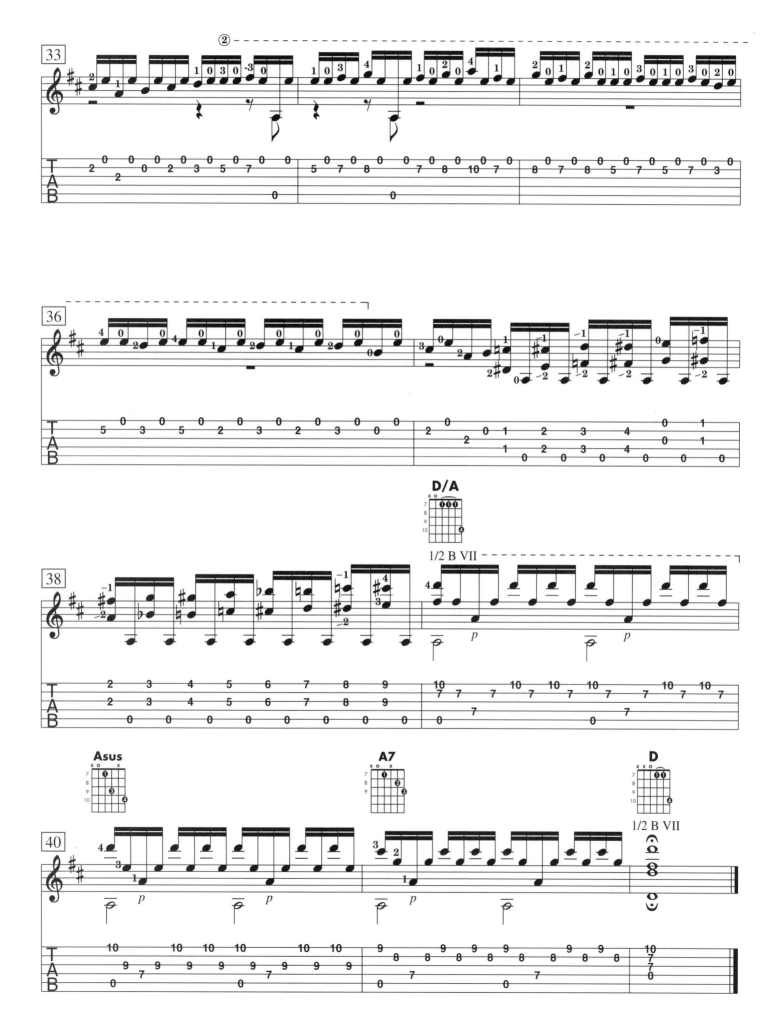

Bourrée

Johann Sebastian Bach (1685–1750)
from the Lute Suite in Em

Gavotte I

Johann Sebastian Bach (1685–1750)
from Cello Suite VI

Jesu, Joy of Man's Desiring

Johann Sebastian Bach (1685–1750)

Study in A

Mateo Carcassi (1792–1853)

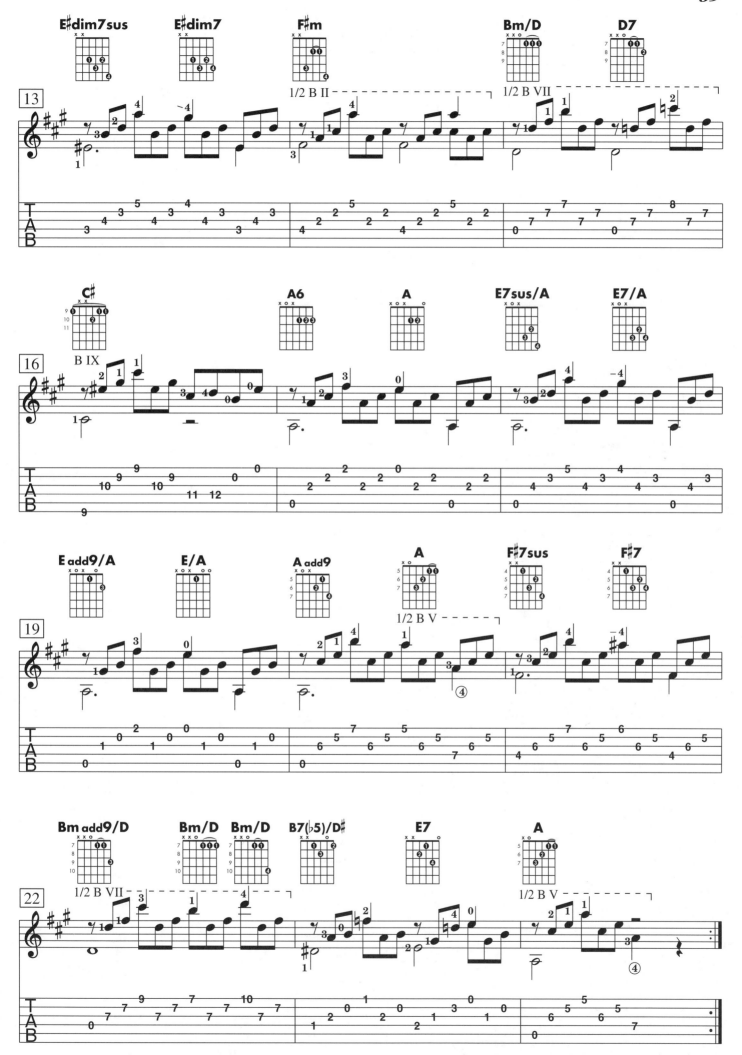

Canon in D

Johann Pachelbel (1653–1706)

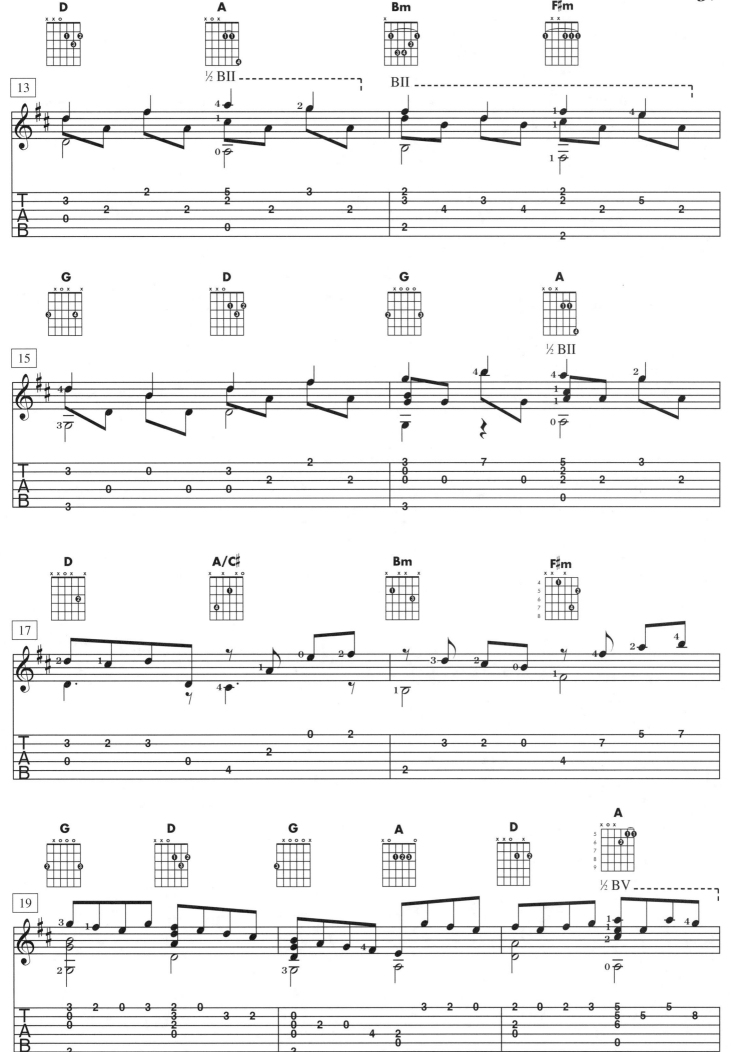

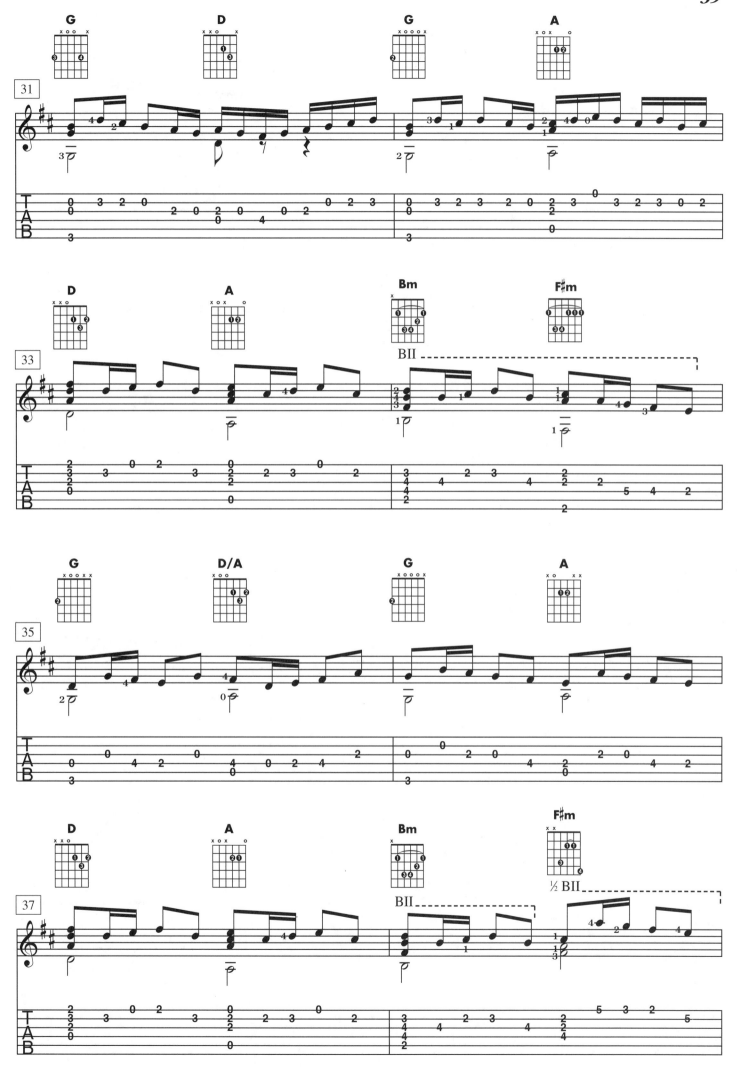

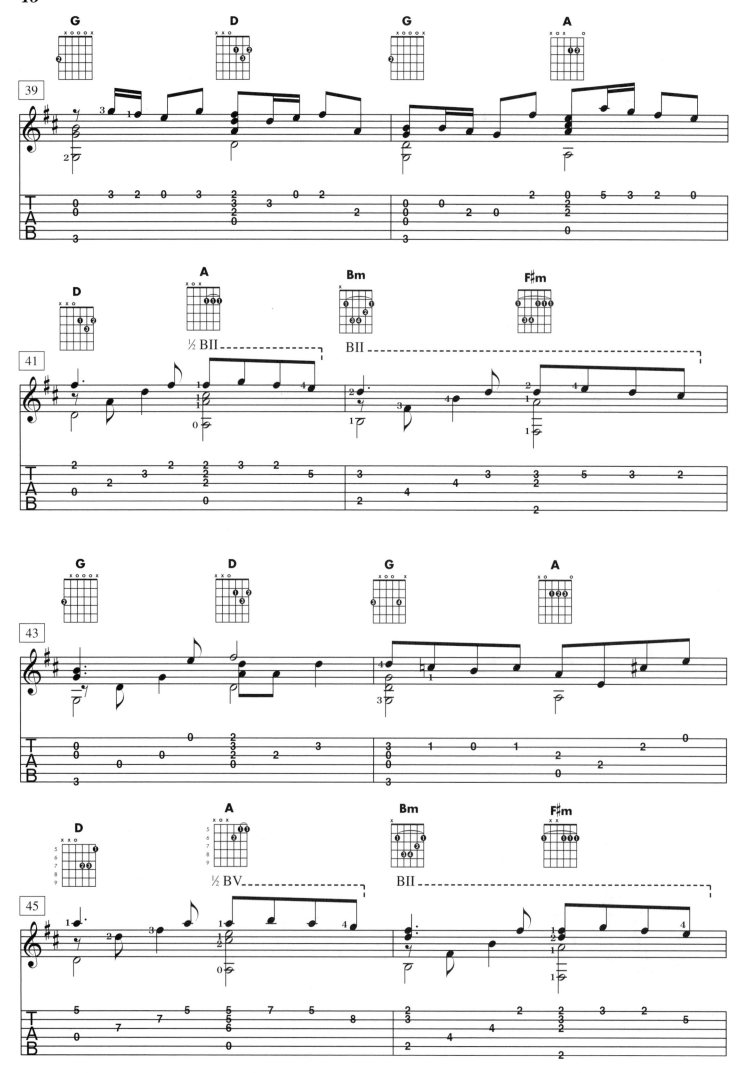

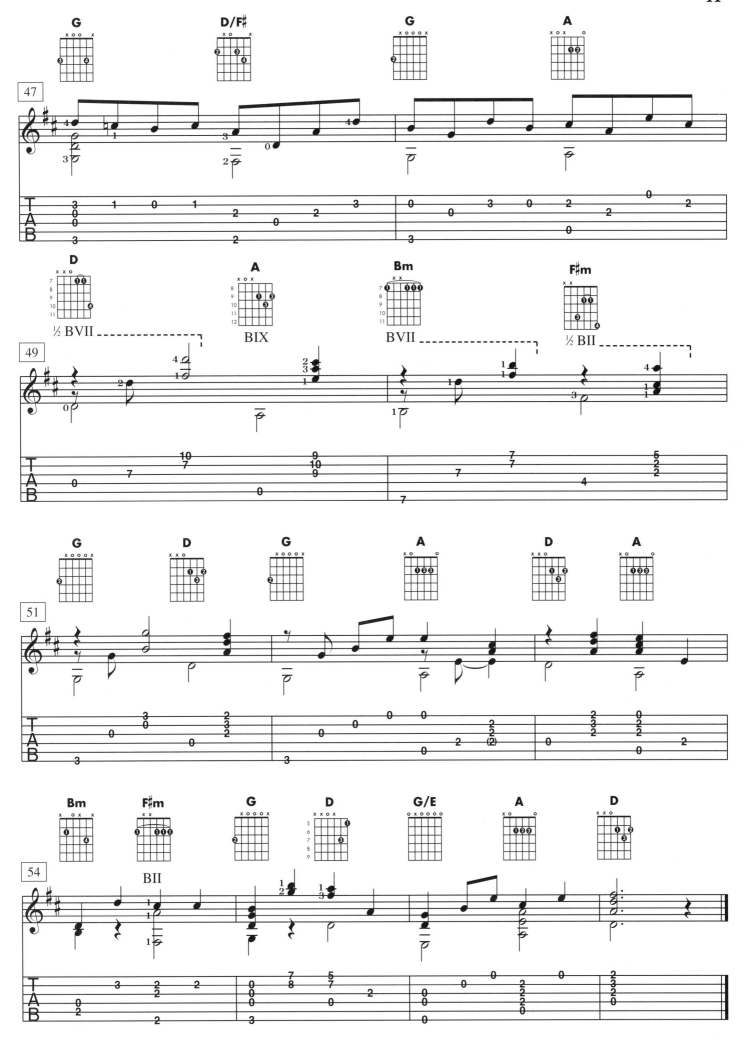

Caprice No. 24

Niccolo Paganini (1782–1840)

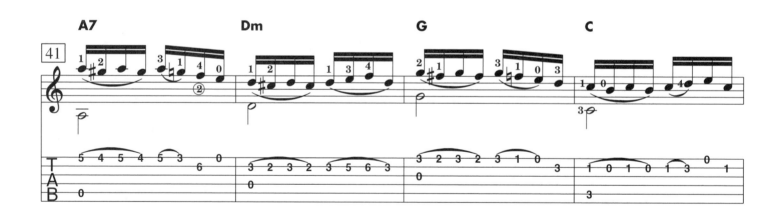

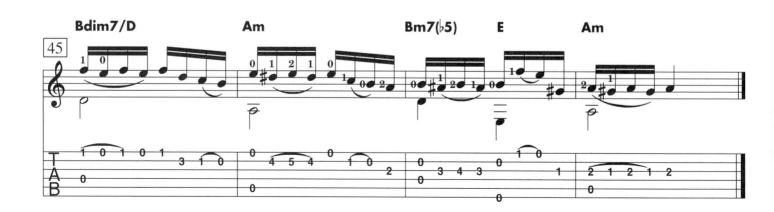

Study in B Minor

Fernando Sor (1778–1839)

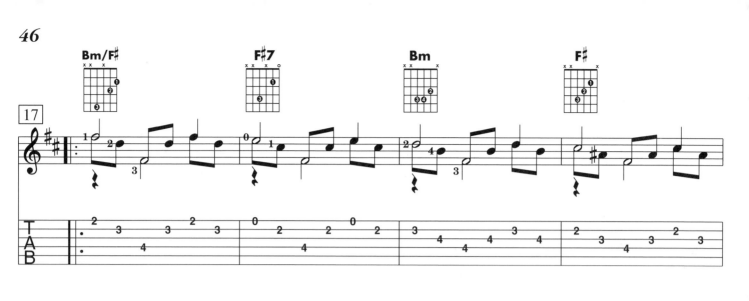

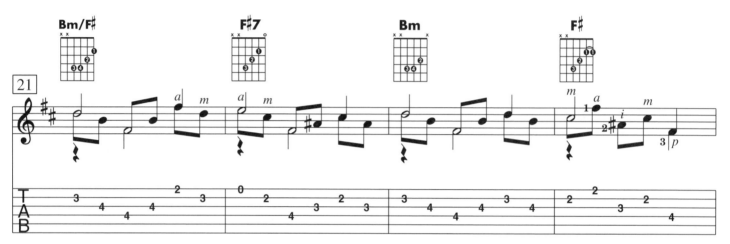

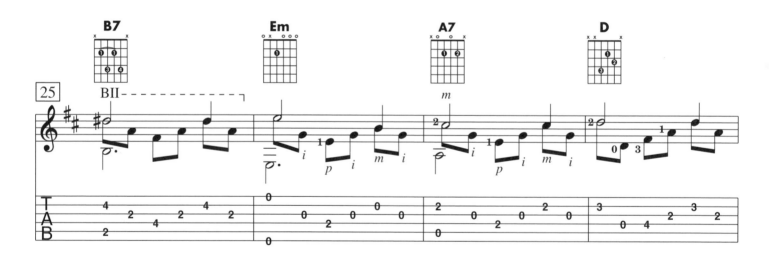

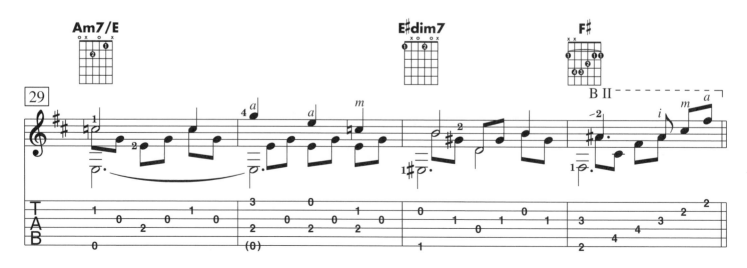

Lagrima (Prelude)

Francisco Tárraga (1852–1909)